Vladimír Holan

Walls

Vladimír Holan

Walls

Verses from years 1932–1977

© Vladimír Holan estate, c/o Aura-pont, 2012
© Translation from Czech: Josef Tomáš, 2012
© Illustrations: Jáchym Šerých, 2012
© Foreword: Jiří Brabec, 2012

*Originally published by Paseka, Praha, 2003, in Holan Spisy 8,
Nocturnál, under the title Zdi*

Typeset in Gramond

Printed and bound in the United Kingdom

ISBN: 978-1-84549-563-3

Published 2012 by arima publishing
ASK House, Northgate Avenue
Bury St Edmunds, Suffolk IP32 6
t: (+44)01284 700321
www.arimapublishing.com

Czech poets in arima publishing

Vladimír Holan
The First Testament, 2005
Soliloquy with Shakespeare, 2007
Narrative Poems I, 2008
Narrative Poems II, 2010
Dolour, 2011
Yet There Is Music, 2012

Jiří Orten
Selected Poems, 2007

Josef Tomáš
The World in My Mouth, 2009

The translation of this book has been kindly subsidized
by the Ministry of Culture of the Czech Republic

Acknowledgement

I am indebted to Clia Goodwin, for her sensitive editing skills
and helpful suggestions in the preparation of these translations.

Contents

Holan's *Walls*

The extensive work of Vladimir Holan contains reflective lyrics, poetic cycles and short stories, lyrical commentaries, prose poems, philosophical compositions, pamphlets, journal entries, prose, and aphorisms. These compositions are situated in specific times and places, differing from one another formally (in one poem we meet a classically regular verse, in the next, a verse that is prosaic), yet always producing an accurately conceived whole.

There is only one collection of poetry that differs in its composition from all his other work: *Walls*, an anthology of those of his previously published verses that are connected by the central motif of its title. The chronological arrangement of the poems allows the reader to recognize that, at first, they concern the exploration of the semantics, or the meaning, of walls, along with the search for meaning related to other motifs that appear frequently in Holan's work. This path towards "fixation"—to anchor imagination, to find something solid in the fleeting world—culminates in the 1930s in the theme of "stone", the material walls are made of. Not surprisingly, his collection from 1937 is entitled *O Stone, you are coming...* . After some years, when characterizing his work from that period, Holan wrote about the path that was "hard, stony" and about the "splitting of a stone". From here, we can follow the direction not only to the "stone of curses" in Holan's war poems, *A Dream* and *The First Testament*, but also to the stony walls behind which he lived for many years in isolation from the public, protesting against the injustices of the Communist regime. In an interview, he mentioned the effect that the time of walls had on his poetry: "It seemed to me quite pointless, after so many years of talking into a wall, to write verses as a dead person for the dead." We read in the poem

A Wall: "Fifteen years I was barred/ and talked but to a wall, / and it's this wall I drag / from within my hell / to let it be the tag / of what is to tell ...". Holan's theme of walls appears in his work not only in the pictures of "a bestialized world", but also in the images of the poet's cruel fate.

The theme of walls is a part of his view of the things that surround us, inside which we live. During all the changes in direction of Holan's life and work, the very word wall gained, for him, an immense breadth of meaning. From the biblical prophet Isaiah, he chose "thy walls are always before my eyes" (here appearing as the epigraph) to reflect the sensory boundaries of the body and the boundaries of existence. This theme of Holan's poetry also reaches the border of poetry and philosophy, and many poems, especially the early ones, strive to capture the philosophical aspect of the poetic tradition. In Holan's work, the theme of walls is also in harmony with his choice of words, his poetic language. The walls of creation, the walls of words that open to vision and hearing are dramatically rendered in small poetic portraits (as of Keats and Homer), and in certain echoes, or responses to the poetry of, for example, Rainer Maria Rilke or William Shakespeare, also implying that his poetry has the dimension of conversation with poets he admires. In this way, the theme of walls touches something that one could call the living space of poesy.

In this sense, Holan's poetry can be described as existentialist. It projects the poetic creativity as a place of lodging, or, as a man's stay in the world and its order. The wall is not only a horizon and a bulwark, a restriction and a protection, but it is also the support of a vision, a projection screen of human destinies—something fleeting on a solid surface. The theme of walls lets us feel Holan's reverence for tradition and order, while keeping in mind the passage of time, when external and internal forces change everything. He senses the metaphysical quality of existence too, a capability of crossing over, of seeing "behind" things, behind this material world, over the wall. In his watchfulness, with his sharp eye, Holan's poetry offers unusual and sometimes paradoxical means: a philosophical reflection and a childlike prattle, an analytical account and a hallucination.

Holan's poetry in this sense is at one time a narrative and at another a breakneck linguistic experiment that in itself embodies the difficulties with expressing what can be seen and experienced in life. In this collection, of course, the place most often used for the poet's reflection is the cemetery wall. It expresses much more than a metaphor for the confines of human life, but it's exactly that wall that opens stunning expanses of what overreaches man, his spiritual dimension, his immersion in the universe in its unfathomable breadth.. Nevertheless, life in Holan's work has a very concrete form. His main interest are the ordinary situations of human life. These diminutive events gain cosmic proportions by the very engagement with fate and by the presence of a seemingly timeless wall, upon which the poet leans, on which he casts his shadow, and which then, second by second, becomes a part of history, of human history.

Vladimír Holan is one of those sovereign poets who saw sharply— in the context of the vastness of a cosmic consciousness of human life—a historicity that has to do with the situation of "being a poet in Bohemia". For Vladimír Holan, and, one can say, for his open universe, this means a difficult search for the meaning of art and poetry in the catastrophes of modern history during wartime and after the war. The wall, so concrete, can carry the metaphor of ascension, be a threshold and still articulate a poetic vision that transcends time and space: "And sometimes, a face bending down appeared,, / which was spurning time so magnificently / that it looked like a hole in the wall of Paradise, / plugged up by the bottom of an angel..."

The wall becomes also that special place between there and here, as if it were shedding , flaking off time between something and nothing: "A beautiful limy wall, which is mirrored in dung water." Bursting through into the miraculous.

Jiří Brabec

... thy walls are always before my eyes.

ISAIAH 49:16

When crossing over from nature to existence,
walls are rather unkind,
walls wet from the urine of talents, walls bespattered
by eunuchs revolting against the spirit, walls not diminished
even though they may not yet be born,
and still walls already rounding out the fruit of the womb ...

A NIGHT WITH HAMLET

TO YOU

I still muse, will she ever come?
And who? And will she sound with joy
on an opalescent epitome
of your kindred, soft and coy?

I still muse, she'll join the roof beams,
dig up a well with a path to the sallow,
and the bees of your voices will suck my themes
out of the roses of words, sweet and mellow –

nothing but themes! For I, at the darkened stress of walls,
know but stones in every part.
It's the feel's form darkness forestalls
in the dark vault of my heart.

THE NOON

All is fed by the desolate
gleam: leaves, a wall, a waterway.
The swan has so funny a gait,
and a wave's spite won't go away.

Only a love too pure
says nothing about man.
Clouds fade in the azure ...
A cloud, then, you should span!

A PRISONER

Oh, to wrench from the sloth the shorter space of the eye!
Like a dog before lying down,
the frame of light whirls from a low sky.

The same pedigree knows the stab wound to take
the day and turn it around
into iron, terminated with a glance into the lake.

An arboreal soul will always sag
in the fight for its southern points ...
Where we love, everything denies any drag.

A leaf fell down to a wall, tears dousing its scars.
And how crumpled are its joints!
Like a man handed to the stars through bars.

A SHADOW, A SHADOW AND A SHADOW ...

Like a dried-up cupboard that lost its key,
fragrance opens up by itself
when you've stepped on silence ...

A thrush pecks at the marzipan of a fence;
a sigh boils over the covered mugs of verdure;
and it doesn't matter, before having swallowed the breeze,
that the music gets burned on a rainbow.

The pansy of time is set on the edge of vibrancy;
the heart is forgiven by something incognito,
till the dry depth from the end of memory
frays into a glare, tickling a dream.

It's only a moment the eye floaters spend in the nooks.
Those in which an insoluble puzzle,
despite all the shakers,
has designs against those who don't exist.

It's by only a moment the steps behind a wall will miss
an end of their never ending search
like the third shoe to a fourth foot –
but it might have been just the frame of a crutch,
uprooted in the joints of mosquitoes,
that caused hearing to limp in the left shadow.

A shadow, a shadow, and a shadow ... And, as it's getting dark,
the park, with an appetite for your head,
can't cope with swallowing the ruffled-up saliva of bird cherry.

NOTHING TO BEGIN WITH

The morgue fattens into a shadow ... And boys
are knocking down plums with bones.
This dual fall with a second-to-none sunstroke
blink briefly through a half-closed ear of vertigo
and then let all the colours die out
into the graveyard's negritude.

Nothing to begin with. Only
the first pause with the second pause
expectorates the blood of music
upon the palm lines, which have
a mere year of space
behind the cracks of walls.

A FUNERAL

Behind a graveyard wall,
from a coffin you stare
at rental deeds' free fall,
leaves in the air.

The rain ascends ... The air
is now wet to its core.
You leave. They play a fanfare
to angels' lore.

Behind a graveyard wall,
they play a tune to graves.
You clear out Miser's Hall
for Grinner's Place.

BY TRAIN

A whistle-stop in a valley. Look: a piece of masonry,
and, like years ago, it still withers away
the trees of beer, the chestnut trees.
And as then, all are only thirds
of scary sounds that have their knives ready.
The penis of a horse turned up his sleeve.
The rain in the door starts feeling womanlike.
A castle in ruins, like a blow to your breast,
and the same air that won't live any further ...

But what I miss here is the child herding flowers
from the railway station garden
to the graveyard of its grandfather.

SUBIDAS

The pulse knocks on the body walls
some stipulated signs.
Imprisoned, we know what each one wants,
we too want all that sounds.

Yet somewhere alone, with no calls
from angels, days and nights,

a saint's breath, full of fire,
knows how to break through any ring.
He destroys his desire
before he's destroyed by suffering.

A NIGHT IN CERNOHOUSY

The whole night they carted wormwood
and shook the wall
under the appearance of sleeplessness.

A twinkling candle diffusively wrinkled
some accidental moments of tranquillity,
especially when the afterthought
blended with the word
into a rhythmical failure of an owl.

Every sound might have to concentrate
if darkness had only its childhood in the space,
until it announced, destitutely constrained
those who are outside are busy!

And they hastened ... The storm-hen
was slowly opening up
above the castle's tower –
and the lightning was mere proof
that the preponderance of observation without love
goes for the images with a knife ...

With every squeal of the farm wagons
you felt the beds of those in limbo
squeaking with the future everywhere else –
and you, infelicitous, asked
where such a birth can be
in which you could find more than some primeval awe ...

BEFORE A STORM

When all turned dark at a bubbling weir,
the swooning blood understood it well
why foamy walls seemed queer
with hemlock's rabietic smell.

As if the wound was missing something,
something that healed, not losing its peace –
an inviting womb seems uninviting
when filled up with the strength of trees.

A woman bites herself into her lover's lips ...

VERSES

The wave, where a fish plays music
from the memory of pebbles,
a graveyard wall on which nappies are dried,
a bird, a falling leaf, a voice somewhere in the fog—
they simplify every gesture,
despite history's pull through nature
eroding the images as far away as to our instincts.

Sorrow responds to the complicated hatefulness
as simply
as when a son
selects the finest words of murder—
and his mother wipes her tears with an apron.

BEHIND

Through dusk, less and less soothing,
the moments walk their pace.
How could a tally count something,
if it's a fading face?

There are answers which tempt
behind the space of daylight.
What's a wall to a saint?
Only for standing upright ...

SUFFERING

In the deceptive air and with a gloomy ruin
of a cloud in the background, a reaper hones his scythe,
as if effacing primeval smudges on the walls of Egbatan
with the soft insides of a loaf.

A fruit, favourably native, is not for us after all,
and any spirituality can hardly set us at ease.
Even perfect attachment still knows suffering;
indeed, the suffering turned familiar with the dead who confide.

LAMENT OF ONE DECEASED

I was allowed to return for a while to my kindred.
Because it was my native province,
the boat-hire place was familiar to me
and I soon arrived at the village.
The wind was helping the air into the sleeves of a weeping
        willow.
It was Sunday, my family was sitting in the orchard,
and only my sister was walking, carrying the milk cans
        into the cellar.
It never occurred to me that I could scare them.
But when they didn't believe it was really I,
I shouldn't have told them that I was alive.
Everything scattered into thin air
with outcries of violets and daisies,
and, in front of me, a cobwebbed landscape was crumbling,
and mezereon and moonlight and an alarm clock
atop a graveyard wall ...

WALLS

It is a town and a night. But a night
that is afraid of dark houses
and of streets pulled down on the flanks of parks.
Another time so much oncoming, it hesitates to advance,
another time so complete and with some extra for itself,
it looks around as if it lost something,
or as if there were something forgotten ...

And truly, in this missed, indebted moment,
it steps nearer and does not yield itself fully until
a little window in the attic lights up
like postage due
on an obituary notice ...

KEATS

But yes, it is he! He who,
inside the poisoned walls of his consciousness,
set on fire the prison yearbook of statues
and, with a revengefully inborn light, taught them to speak
words left out by the first day after the world's creation ...
Alas, he was allowed to do so only for a lustreless
and yet truly superfluous moment,
because to underground gods and dogs
juvenility is true only inside the child
who, mute and blind, is already dead inside its mother ...

Space roars, with its chin in the palm of nothingness,
and it is in the one place only where
the flattened deplored scent of an abandoned vermouth
and the gate to a slaughterhouse, bulged out like Homer's eye,
lurk ...

ONE SINGLE PIECE OF HISTORY

I used to stand more than once (when one could drink God
and the devil could not be slept out),
I used to stand more than once at the little windows of night
       pharmacies
and lend my ear to all pleas, all sighs,
all questions and all thanks, to all openings of hearts,
and worries and anxieties, discoloured by frequent washing
       in tears
and by humiliation in front of shameless hope –
and I used to feel wafting through that wild-looking
       little window
both vexation and kindness and, other times, irritation
of an effervescent being in a white coat of never-ending
       waking up,
and the scent of miser's lilies, and also a surplus
of colourless poisons, which were handed out
only against the pawn tickets of possible recovery,
which, alas, in advance,
sold the eyes of all sickly men to emptiness –
and I used to see in that little window,

always, the one hand watchful and the other drowsy,
one motherly and the other unconcerned,
but each of them trembling, and as if fried
in the oil from Solomon's lamp ...
And sometimes, a face bending down appeared,
which was spurning time so magnificently
that it looked like a hole in the wall of Paradise,
plugged up by the bottom of an angel ...

Then as heavy as a pocket carrying the stones of maledictions,
all the more dolefully and fully in disfavour,
I used to be on the point of a desire to hear
the voice of the first-born rooster,
and, soon afterwards, the forenoon creeping up
when the shouting of playing children
restrains sadness as red flies do at a funeral ...

A WALL

A beautiful limy wall, which is mirrored in dung water,
receives from eternity more than the stone upon a crypt.
Without conclusion, without cognition and yet warmly,
it lives between God and humankind,
and its sole outspread crack
is looked upon, from God's side, by a horse,
and, from the men's side, by a protruding horse shaft.

A beautiful and cruel wall!

AT A VILLAGE GRAVEYARD AT THE WALL
OF SELF-MURDERERS

Here, where sneezeweed kisses the photograph of the
        deceased,
and where the nun of a tombstone keeps the stained
        movement of marble
within the cackle of geese ... oh yes, exactly here
everything assents as well that man was not created
but made. Things also were only made.
Man and things, made for the reproof of the dead.
Things wait. Man surmises.
Things beseech. He resists.
Things grow old and linger on. He is immortal and dies away.
Things are forsaken and he is lonesome,
and he is not lonesome only in so far
as his life is turning against itself ...

A WALL

A wall ... A wall so spiritual that it can now only abase,
a wall that withholds from a tempted soul any motion,
and from the motion nostalgia for breaking through into
        the miraculous,
yet a wall that is somehow humiliated by the mystery
of why it stays here at all—and balancing this feeling
by being so tall and not crumbling ...

AT A CEMETERY

When, outside, petty life strives and aspires,
and when, just behind the wall, a child carries some sausages
        from the market
and sits down in the bushes and smells them covetously
but mustn't eat even a single one
because they are counted—
here, as the story goes, all is asleep ...
It is, however, nothing more than an imposed sleep,
and the stones here are like the dentures
that people take out before narcosis,
telling their dear ones in the waiting room:
"No need to stay here, I am going to scream!"
But they don't scream, and as much as we like to stay with them,
there is always someone who leads us, sobbing, away,
leads us away into life, which struggles and strives,
except that it's into a life whose gifts
disgust us more and more,
because they have been counted ...

SHROVE TUESDAY

In the decrepit plaster of the town, shaken by the song
            of nothingness
like a decoration in an opera house,
in a disreputable habit of pedestrians,
walking blindfolded outside themselves,
in the movement of fingers that imitate centipedes
as centipedes imitate the spines of sardines,
in walls turning cloudy,
in which there are more windows than children,
and in the air, which likes the blue colour,
he chooses grey, and black is the result.
Yes, in everything that can't multiply fate into simple love
by insults, anxiety, and impoverished suffering,
a single sunray appears,
illuminating a baby pram,
which could not fit into the tram any more ...
And at the same time someone asks Galileo: "Is the sun eternal?"
And he answers: 'Eternal? No! But very old!'

THIS TOO

This too is your lot: to witness bitterly lewd silence
and just at those moments when only the Underworld knows
what a woman dares before a man decides,
both right in the middle between the fallen tree of youth
        and the excrement of an old age.
This too is your lot:
bitterly to witness the adulterous lechery of music,
exactly at those moments when, she, pushed into her crotch,
thrusts forth her breasts
so as to sough then from her nefarious mouth
through the wall cracked by Agamemnon's fall to you ...

REMBRANDT

Rembrandt perceived it ... and he knew
that a chipped wall, a cracked grape, a woman-woman
who are not here as an abyss
cannot be a sign.

Rembrandt knew it ... and he felt that
the decision that the plainest dish,
served on the most expensive plate,
is always near an ideal
in the lustre of a mortuary fly.

Rembrandt perceived it ... And he knew
that souls are between themselves and their selves
so that they might not escape from themselves,
but that genius is an unceasing presence ...

A GRAMOPHONE RECORD

"That record is broken!" says a demonic voice ...
and truly, a black-golden ray of nothingness
gets stuck in the crack between God and men,
a prickle of insecurity scrapes at the crack in a graveyard wall,
and the sting of mystery scratches the crack in a woman.

We play ... We play catch with time,
but everything goes on turning ... From here arrives
our consciousness, the consciousness of mere appearances ...

TWO OF THEM

Two stars on the forehead of a sky-born cow
pull themselves down into themselves by their overripe
        heaviness
so that later, when falling, they can mingle
Apollo's parabola with the nape of a drunkard
and steer into the diamond shire of Mallarmé ...

Even if we overtake consciousness, we screen ourselves
        by inspiration.
And so, in the intimate rays of the two stars' light,
one can glimpse only the wall of a seedy gooseberry bush,
where two women chuckle without knowing why,
and when squatting, they look at each other and urinate ...

IN THE PROVINCE

Your eye, etched by the last buttercup,
twinkles with blissful but impatient pain
and throws then, in front of itself, the first stage of the evening.
The sunset is plain. There is nothing in it
that could baffle a potato road
leading straight into a village
above which smoke rises
with a promise that supper is being prepared ...
A few figures stand under a walnut tree
that catches the motion of their hands
as they talk about black horses with loose shoes.
A few rapid sounds, softly bitter
like a piece of lint on thighs,
open themselves into warm walls ...
And that's all ... and yet, who could deny
that it does not concern buildings, but cottages,
and thus not houses, but homes? ...

A SUNDAY AFTERNOON AT A PRAGUE SUBURB

Sultry heat, walloped with a golden bag, is splitting
this stinking suburb with dizziness
as far as the consciousness of the street,
where today, at last, someone appears
who a long time ago, walked out from burnt Ilium.
How firm he is in his youth!
And yet, despite all his self-confident silence,
with seven lips on seven leaves of kissing,
and despite all his self-confident radiance, knowledgeable
of the crosscut through a brick wall, and concentrated
upon an obstinate entrance –
he looks like an approximate one ...
This may be because he is wearing a ready-made suit,
or because he is not ruthless enough to recognize
that he is reaching his goal.
But yes! he has entered,
and he will soon see that an abattoir,
still uses dross for bedding mute creatures ...

A PREMONITION

On a December night, you filled up the glass of your hard
            drinking with wine
and went away into the adjacent room for a book ...
When you returned, after a while, the glass was half empty.
Swallowing your fear through the glottis of insanity,
you asked who had taken a sip from it, since you were living alone,
erratically surrounded with the thorny stone of walls,
and you asked about it with such a barbarity that you repelled,
now long ago, both the statue, and the monster, and the ghost ...

A VOICE

At dusk, as venomous as January
around the house which one heats with lignite coke,
in the street where some snot,
just now freely flicked out by a boy,
gives evidence about the road to the reformatory
at dusk,
where snow is suspected of a barber's towel
that fell out from a ragman's dosser of thaw,
between the walls built up by a drunkard's grief
from red blots on the face of dead poets.
And you suddenly heard the following:
However black may be the soul, it can hardly persuade the body
about the needlessness of life, unless a self-murderer doesn't
        believe in soul.
And then, in order to deserve this disbelief,
the soul would have to kill itself earlier than the body would do ...
And it can't do that because it didn't give itself life.

A RESORT

Some time ago, it was a bathhouse ... Today, not even the wind
        loiters about;
also those leached jackdaws hardly remember
the tennis shorts, scalded to their last thread,
and the pitfalls of female garters ...
And, of course, not even evil spirits are there
because they were banished long ago to waterless places;
here they would only batten on dampness and mildew,
where there is no difference between the roof and the floor ...

Only the walls, aglomerated like a gunshot
and collapsing halfway down to their waists,
uncloak a hunchback in the innyard there,
who, attired in clothes left by the dead Strauss,
chopped down all the trees and all the bushes
to ensure that, in the autumn, he doesn't have to sweep up
fallen leaves ...

A STOPOVER OF A COURIER

If there were snow, a footprint would remain after me,
here, where for a while I lean on the wall of a hemp kiln ...
All, however, feels warm and greenish.
Even women have made up their faces with malachite,
Rye turns yellow, clouds grow heavy
and the pond mirrors them like morphine under the skin ...

The papyrus from Oxyrhynchus is, in fact, too young
in comparison with what I am carrying ... Is a war coming
        again ...?

How silently a horse drinks ...

THOSE OTHERS

A cemetery chapel, seen over a garden wall
where a cat devours a nightingale,
such was my vision of life.
I lived through it and don't know why I should offer
any apologies to whomsoever of the mortals.

Even the most unreserved declaration of love
is like a downfall of all living beings at once.
Even the most voiceless declaration of love
is like a resurrection of all graves at once.

Those others are coming to me, those others ...

ONLY OVER THE WALL OF A BONEYARD

This hermitage, where man used to cut his hair crosswise
to oust his sinful thoughts,
this hermitage, a womb, not fed
unless with a cord around its loins,
this hermitage, a throat, waiting
for a ritual knife used for cutting off one's breath,
this hermitage, where an angel is carved into sandstone
sitting on top of a rooster and the rooster on top of a skull,
this hermitage, completely apart from itself, corresponds
to a poet's fame only over the wall of a boneyard ...

MORS ASCENDIT PER FENESTRAS

It may be that demons can pierce through walls,
it may be that Death really enters through windows,
but only Jesus Christ could enter through a closed door,
and then only to the Apostles ...

Our one and only Guardian Angel comes not, leaves not.
He is with us all the time, faithful to us
and human in his compassion. He is with us all the time,
with me already for almost fifty years—and yet,
not until today, did it cross my mind, while drinking wine,
that I have never invited him
to have a drink with me ...

REMEMBRANCE OF SEPTEMBER 1952

The itch of an autumnal wall,
scratched to the blood of a thicket creeper ...
What a wonder that you, Czech poet, don't beg ...
But, to rely on man
is like not believing in God
and still wanting a miracle ...

AN AUTUMN NIGHT

A couple of trees, still green, are abreast with the acidity
of a park, defoliated long ago,
because the sharp scent of its whiskey
is already in the second still.

The finger alphabet of a deaf-mute is not as mad
as the moon, which takes concern in so many sunrays
that one of them is adequate.

Yet somewhere behind an illicit tapestry,
someone has already drained a glass
without touching it with his lips.

Yet somewhere behind a wall,
harmonious with the flight of woodlice,
a man lies, requiring what's due
from an absent woman ...

ALONG THE WAY

Leaning against a tree, which is afraid of lightning,
you feel that there will be lots of apples this year.
A couple, Adam, in a virgin just yesterday,
laughs and, with a one-year-old branch, drives away
the flies from around bovine eyes.
In a nearby flour mill, a millstone runs.
The brook, fleetingly swollen by rain,
intimately presses upon you to stay.
It is really lovely here,
and lovely also is the visible shouting—
but why is it always children who love to climb
over a graveyard's wall? ...

A WALL

Why is your flight so hard,
and why does it stall
Fifteen years I was barred
and talked but to a wall,

and it's this wall I drag
from within my hell
to let it be the tag
on what is to tell.

THE END OF YOUR SCHOOL YEAR

The end of your school year caught up with you
in the waiting room of God. Despite being almost
in your sixties, compared with the One who is your father,
you are still a child ... But then,
instead of vacations, you came there
with all your ailments ...
Woe is you! The ailments were without love for Him.
You were told that He was not admitting.

Who told you so?
The walling-in told you ...

FAITHFULNESS

What is here is faithful: a wall that gives fresh air,
but it's not doing it alone
because the statue it carries
is aerating too ...

How then to fail to remember
what will happen when the Universe,
on the run from itself,
meets itself!

IT SHOULD BE HERE ALREADY

Crows fly away. A pen scrapes.
The rain translates clouds into the language of walls.
A horse begins its chest in music.
Women are aware of all the clothes
they were wearing from their childhood to their maidenhood
and across their blood further on.
The fall of rebellious angels hesitates
about what to do with the resurrection
that the instinct of insects ruled out ...
But the night should be here already
because, for hungry eyes,
the moon looks like a pancake
spread over a whole plate ...

AND AGAIN TO YOU—KAREL HYNEK MÁCHA

I

How little we know about him ... Could it be
that he was too close and we could not withdraw?
And that he was regenerating himself without change?
That we considered his hidden motives
as some impermanent and only accidental madness?
He used to say that it was necessary to set limits
upon the freedom of prison walls
because they have now begun to be everywhere.

And we thought that it was to his advantage
when he alone, from his childhood in prison,
was allowed to close the door behind himself
and then throw the keys through the window
to the executioner ...

II

It is, however, possible that he wanted only to say
that it did not strike him like that,
because if we are only for ourselves,
why do we want any action?
It is, however, also possible
that we were waiting for someone
who was just coming out of his prison,
but even this was quite unreliable ...

III

And that we are afraid ...that we are afraid
of our internal images only because
they arrive at their forms through our deepest sensuality,
and it is the forms that put an end to any growth.

I hear how death devours a soul's roar.

AN ASSASSIN

No closer to you, no farther from you am I,
than it is from Cappadocia to a bawdy house
where a wall paints on its stone
two kinds of dresses of the third body,
and where jealousy
cannot be only a premonition anymore
in everything that it did not bring to fruition,
no closer, no farther.

So it will be here and now ...

JUST ONLY WE

A broad-hipped hill, a bosomy wall and a tower so real!
It's only we, accidental, ephemeral,
who are here like phantoms,
if not for any other reason than just because
we are answering ourselves with something
that was most absent in the question.

We are afraid.

THAT ONE TOO

What was left alone,
not by those not present at the moment
but by those who are not any of them—
even without allusions about the clatter of shackles,
even without any regard for everyone's talking
about the same thing, but everyone in a different way:
all that too has the walls that are closer than partitions.
Nothing is here while you wait.
This will be lost in death too,
and well before you die ...

AT FOUNDATIONS

Today, in fact, only dismay
follows the truth
along false trails of hide-and-seek.
Permanent is the horror too. Oh, poetry,
if it were not for you,
I would get used to that; thus I would destroy that
and would not live.

Why are they walling up that window opposite?

ABYSS OF AN ABYSS

This place is a wasteland ... Its
inviolacy, and so its virginity ...
Close to it, the one and only wall is leaning
in order to fall or to watch closely
whether, still during the life of death,
the earth is accepted through perpetually giving birth ...
This does not involve only lovers, but, surely,
their dissimilarity intrinsically abates
the access of the withdrawal ...

A WALL

For you were there with me
less abundant than one.
And for the earth said: "A wall
is not for reaching up the height ... This one
is the wall of a distillery, covered with vomit
straight up from the foundation stone —
and another, the one close to the church door
moves the passing-bell's tower away ..."

WITH A QUESTION

What's here is a wall, a venerable wall!
Oh, how it is on its own!
Then it has no need to repeat itself
in order to start with an appeal
and to renounce any evocation.
It's only you, although merely old,
who bumped yourself against it with a question,
to what extent is the devil free ...

ANOTHER WALL

What's here is a wall ... A wall, with the light
opposite the desolated steps of an echo,
is on the left hand of the moon. In a fiery way,
one can avoid it. In a burnt-out way,
it is already excluding itself by lacking any exclusion.
And yet, how much you like to lean against it,
because it was not built from any more stones
but from the stones of the future.

AMOR FATI

The reason for expecting you, though you are so close,
is also the wall I still know nothing about
by how many fingers it is here from the ends of bodies,
so the souls cannot get out.

To honour lifeless things is only for those
who can but yearn when they desired;
and so we really are both alone, not acting
because it already had once happened.

THE RAIN

The rain falls on a Whitsun of dogs
and changes the beauty of bitches ...
Peasants are dying behind walls
and don't know what they will give
before they say goodbye, because love
still marches backwards for them ...
This will end badly ... Even in those villages
that are so close to each other
that they would gather at the whistle of a train ...

WITHOUT

Without showing herself, she went away
through the other door of her innocence.
Next to this door and together with it,
the draught of walls distorts us
towards the woe, alone and one,
which, because of the closeness of existence,
did not show anticipation of any inevitability.
That's how children die. I do not understand.

FEAR

There is no such road that would lead somewhere else
unless one would be allowed to go farther,
but just there, there is a fence, a wall,
or an assassin ... The fog too
is to the giving earth and the withdrawing heaven
a chip of kindling wood that went out at their encounter ...
What to do with the soul without a body? ... Feelings
live an exalted secret to keep tears from falling down ...

FOR THE OTHERS

For the others who will come, it will be
only a change of a hint and a road,
free of horse apples, free of a wall
showing saltpeter sprouting over, free of tax
levied on the brothel's chimney ... Something
added to the very first bleakness ... But,
like self-delusion, in no way ever more free,
it will remain and will slander itself
by itself with a captive deception ...

A WALL

This wall is not here because of longer boughs
full of fruit there on the inner side behind it ...
It does not separate, it does not guard, it does not judge
and, being old, it is aware
of intervening with silence
by crumbling as far as the very bloodstone ...
And because it cannot be anything else,
it misses nothing, even if it signs off
as a rarely frequented female toilet ...

THE END?

The autumn ... Perhaps the last one,
with the last apple from the Tree of Knowledge ...
Ecce, the time when one cannot wait
till a colour redeems itself, till a painting dries ...
Ecce, the time when emptiness and thirstiness,
under a light without warmth
and yet as if waiting for accomplishment,
destroy wickedness, felony and life ...

All that appears on the wall too,
the wall efflorescent with saltpeter, the wall
so close to falling over that, at the end, nobody is here ...

IN THE WORMWOOD

By shifting walls and drawing aside
boughs, mayflies and clouds,
you've found today a playground left by dead children ...
It was already in disrepair, overgrown, and asking
for the last sympathy, and so somehow
smaller and as if brought to bay ...
But, in the wormwood and dead nettles,
a rolled-away ball was buried ...
And a pearl button was there too ...
And the whole moon was needed
to bath it in rays ... Don't cry ...

A WALL

This wall with a hurriedly closed
bit of space is also
full of reddish cracks
after its bricks suffered a paralytic stroke ...
Little attentive to the absence of the sun,
shadows hide an understanding with man
given the intrigue ...
And right here, my lady, you have asked me
whether life is a dream, you,
so alive at the moment of sleeping,
fully inside your dream ... But the wall!
Did it come to consciousness of itself?

THE LAST ONE ?

The wall here is like the last one
because one is forbidden to go farther.
High enough to protect a secret,
but still so shabby
that it allows taking a look through its cracks
and to see behind what lay in front:
a wooded incline of the wind, a rye field, and a lark.

If cognition is death, what to do with cognition
regenerated by death?

MURATA

Over the wall that absents its foundation,
one could even feel as reaching deep
and also as overcoming all
that stays, mutually and diametrically,
in one's way and has nothing to say to oneself ...
But it is possible
that the wall thus meant nothing
and that, from the accidental to the excessive,
there is so much time for a sleep
that its time does not have to be interrupted ...

REALLY

It was not that it went dark, because
darkness is everlasting.
And as it doesn't know what's coming
after it, it is also idle.

And so, we, the blind are here:
groping among perceiving walls,
because even what's inside us
is out of our reach ...

A WALL

You barely stepped forward,
and a wall is here already, with
a statue of death on it,
well fed by the baroque ... If that's your feeling,
you could stay in its shadow
overnight, and nothing
would be denied you ... If that's
your cognizance, don't stop yourself
inside your double, but retreat
into your suffering ...

A WALL

It is just a piece of a wall
nurtured by its sadness and with its heart
eaten by the urine of phantoms who
then climb over it ... Yes, but
onto which side, when
they always argue
whether their nature lies
here or somewhere else? ...

FOR THE LIFE OF ME

A wall ... made out of love for an orchard
and out of hate for people.
On its inward side, there are more trees
than fruit. On its outward side,
there are more sins than thighs.
This wall, despite being strong and tall
and pointed, entices after all.
For the life of me, in its cracks,
there lie vipers in wait. A good wall!

THIS ONE TOO

That Kallikrates was building long walls
is also testified by this short little wall,
its building suddenly stopped, which,
to guard its mystery,
says nothing about what there was from the beginning.
You may circumnavigate it and look at it
from the other side too. But,
even if the very eternity
of anything here in this world is affected by change,
you won't escape suffering …

YOU, WOMAN ...

You can't remember any more. I can.
The swelter was on the verge of falling down,
shirts lifted up, black to a fault;
a rowan at the well, till now always
an audible silence in any
form of a shadow; to the left a wall,
desolate as a thought without its image;
some bushes, which could not
come closer than a halfway;
and then a window into the yard where they feasted
on altar plates taken
from neighboring churches ... But
you don't remember any more, although
it's just the women who spread gossip.

SECRETLY

Even days, odd days ... Are they really
more important than evenings and nights
when delight without cruelty seems
to be without love? Unless it might have been
on the day of the Virgin Mary's Espousal ... Unless
it would have been just at that moment
when, pampered by pain, we ask:
"Are you behind the wall? Behind yours or mine?"

O Bastardello, it's possible to live
also with murderers
just in order to live. And also
even a thing given as a gift
can be stolen ...

AND VERY NEAR

"Look," he said, "The Plague Cemetery,
and it is larger than Denmark! Several trees
have reason to softly enhance
its underlying, mountainous content. Remotely
and somehow innocently overlooked,
little squares of spindle weed live out of wedlock
with wild hops. The low wall too
did not miss anything that would detach it
from the goose girl on the stubble field.
And very near that low wall, there lies,
and still waits to be alone at last,
the pre-Hamlet Shakespeare
of a post-Shakespeare Hamlet …"

AGAIN

Without being able to hope
it is so far!
Without being able to realize
that you lament so much,
the neighbor already bangs on the wall!
What choice do you have but to return again,
to recognize again, and to refuse again?

AN AGED ONE

A wall, a pulled-down wall ... They started,
not before it dawned, somewhat inconveniently,
wildly and scowling ... Perhaps for the reason
that it disappointed, was past its service, even interfered,
that it had no chance to retreat,
that it despised itself,
and that therefore it would take
its own runaway life ...
that aged, warm, and yet
exasperating argillite wall!

STAINS

A wall, a chipped wall,
as if not able to do
without a free revival in its heart,
but curious all the time about
what stains, mold, and the most frequent cracks
are capable of ... It is its melancholia,
not yours, that you, when passing by,
carress it here and there, even though
you know well that it may be only stone
that does not have to be reborn, new from old ...

A wall, a chipped wall ...
Far behind it, people are in a hurry,
and everyone knows both the direction and the place,
but no one knows
which way and where to ...

HERE AND THERE

A wall. A cemetery wall. In disrepair
and trampled down thoroughly by the shoes
of urchins who climb over it
to find the ball they kicked
between the graves ... Its
privilege to be unusual,
and therefore redundant, is over,
and yet still here
for unfulfilled dreams. These
overlap, but the wall shrinks
and is already almost invisible,
yet it is still possible
to have a glimpse of it here and there ...

WHY

Storms and lightning abuse
bovine eyes somewhere in the stable
and, wanting, furthermore, to make some lithographs,
they wait for the continuation of walls ...

Only you, in front of the closed gates
and boarded-up windows,
ponder even, while walking,
why a virgin has not appeared for so long,
for it is not in the heart
what could not have happened,
as if it were for the first time ...

THAT WALL

Then they talked about another thing,
but not in another way ... And exactly then,
you suddenly saw that wall;
the wall all grown up somewhat of necessity,
even though, by the secret sign
of whores, pimps and cops,
the wall actually quite
recent, with a license permit,
and so not for long, the wall
that, despite everything, as if begging
for its own destruction ... But if not
for its request having been definitive,
it would be reaching even further ...

THE WALL THAT BUILT ITSELF ALONE

Restless lightning, excessive clouds,
and, below, the earth
drowned by a gale. But at
the most receptive place
is the wall that built
itself alone, and in such a way
that it could not do otherwise.
The wall does not avoid the suspicion
that, when necessary,
it will collapse from an unexpected
oversight, just as truly as
it does not object at all to staying here
ad nauseam ... But how many
secret entrances are in it
for the beings who retired their fate!

AN ATELIER

Have I called this a myth? Why not?
It was this alone that,
at first, as if on purpose,
reached later as far as a pensive mood
that would live here in its own ways ...
However, be that as it may (and don't believe
that walls and surrounds are doing it),
when you are in a barn,
you can take a detour around nothing ...
And so everything which I have here
is not inconsistent with that
which surrenders at first sight ...
You know, there is no need of an empire's fall,
to cause many things to crack,
including oilcloth ...
And then, when one thing blends
with the other, you never ask
about the background ...

EVEN THIS IS A WALL

It is as clear as daylight
that even this is a wall,
even if with its head down
or close to a collapse,
and thus nothing more than an underpinning ...
But whether in sleep or
in exile, nothing
can escape its watchfulness,
although it hardly accords
with what it leans against,
for it is a wall
that stands by the river,
and water takes away ...

WALL AS A SELF-PORTRAIT

From this wall, once prepared
for a mural, there remains today
only an enclosure of planks
looking as if ashamed,
but, at the same time, as if nothing
had happened ... Leaning on it
(be it under the Chaldean
or the Czech sky), someone told you:
"You were a nuisance to yourself
straightaway at the first meeting,
even if this had not been
from so close then!"

TWO WALLS

It's the wall of a mill and the adjacent
wall of a barn that change both places
into a citadel, almost animal-like
in its self-defense ... A citadel ...
But not to leave the very unexpected
in doubt,
there sneak in for full centuries,
and out of some kind of rashness,
just those lovers
who were to see each other never again
because they did not recognize each other ...

THIS IS THAT WALL

This is that wall onto which
(in the least expected moment
and as if he only wanted to surprise)
a man sick to death knocks
and does not make himself heard ... Perhaps
because it is just he who once
refused to live as two decided
to become double and thus go alone against himself.

The wall is a witness ...

KAMPA

These lanes are not
visited out of habit
and therefore don't evoke an identical impression.
One gets lost in them, and it is they,
where gas lamps still illuminate
the pavement, somewhat freshly damp
either from the night dew
or the urine of drunkards ...
The lanes, where shadows of shadows,
thrown by ancient walls,
do not attempt a plot but only scene,
which seems surprising for them alone ...

A suitable moment when you do not know
what comes next ...

THIS WALL

Not that it would be disruptive to doubt,
or that it would remember in a bad way,
but this wall needs a support.
Well, they do it,
lovers and drunkards –
and you feel that to withdraw your
even if not helping,
at least comforting, hand
would be here as equally offensive,
as to withdraw it when making a toast
or after having been asked to kill ...

THE STRAIGHT WALL

The corner of a lane, almost a hump, ashamed
for the straight wall that extends
as far as the garden, where right now
viburnum and geranium are in bloom
and where children play and therefore speak
neither about themselves nor about others ...

When a guard reproaches them
about their dirty little collars,
they answer, "Well, it's only Saturday!"

A NEW WALL

A wall, a new wall, somehow built hastily,
pretending and actually
so mendacious that you would prefer
looking for a ruin.
Right next to it, up to the edge of the asphalt,
there is a bus stop
and a station of taxi drivers.
And just one of them, leaning on that wall,
skinny and somewhat not knowing
whether he lives during his break or is
on vacation or in retirement,
asked you whether Jesus Christ
was baptized at all ... You know,
baptized as a child!
"How young is your child?" you said.
"A little over two years," he said.
"Let him be baptized!" you said ...

THE WALL OF A CEMETERY

And what can one see over this
wall of a cemetery? The sun,
a little worn out, a clothes-line,
foreign tourism and a tram,
which, too, ride always to the terminus.
And inside the wall, there is a burial.
And the dead one, though he keeps silent by himself,
cannot be present...

A DESOLATE WALL

A wall, a desolate wall, the wall of a widower.
And as if resolved
to say it straight, but not aloud,
it desires something similar:
a second wall, and behold! an echo is here ...
Then the man who knows
why he was frightened
feels up to his liver of adultery
that only a little later
his deceased wife appears there,
if she wants, if need be ...

A WALL

Everything seemed to indicate
that we, when so late,
and having no alternative
to talking, should spend the night in this barn,
the emptiness of which required no entrance fee
as if holding off for
what wasn't here before. But we
immediately fell asleep. And it was the one,
that age-old, beautiful barn,
which wanted to whisper something to us,
or even keep silent about it
in order to make it clearer,
however ... But exactly then,
a bat rose up flying,
looking for the door, till now always open,
which we closed not long ago ...

A PORTRAIT

While pondering whether to write
something into the album of her little cousin,
or walk the dog,
she decided neither to support aging,
nor to water nor iron her clothes,
nor to hear the voice of a newsboy on the stairs,
nor to hear the door slam
but to remain between bare walls ...
To make this happen, she began
to roast larks on a spit ...
That was how you caught her,
and you were scared then ... That's also
why most of the sculptures are beside themselves ...

FOR MEDITATION

Walls of stone, walls of clay,
door closed ... Except that it is
the closed door that is wide open ... Or
is it somewhere else like a gateway now,
wide closed? Sometimes, when threatened,
we help ourselves by walling in all of them ...

A BRICK WALL

A wall, a brick wall ... When they parted,
he said to her: "It was not for your voice,
for your words, for your speech, no,
but always when you were succumbing
to nothingness that you were more honest
than the one who loves ... "

And yet, he almost considered
what he concealed as self-denial ...

A SHABBY WALL

A cemetery wall, an almost suspiciously
shabby wall, through the holes of which
pigs enter to graze the grass on the graves ...
To a pilgrim, it appears as if he wrote
in his last will that he was broke ...
It is, however, possible that he is surprised,
and that he is wrong ...

NO WAY TO GO

When rats cough and scrape lime
off the walls to eat it,
you don't feel that your solitude is so barren.
It's harsher when Fate, suddenly unrecognizable,
concurrently frets over whether He is a nuisance,
not being allowed to do what He pleases,
not knowing whether He will still be bold enough
to hide, beyond recognition,
that He misses someone
and that He took a dislike against Himself,
and that He is contemptuous of Himself! ...

THE WALL OF THE HOUSE OPPOSITE

After today's downpour, there came to the fore,
in particular, the wall of the house opposite.
Not without cause because,
though only half rainswept,
it now donates more than it has,
and it does at times when it least expects.
It's a wall of a brothel,
the wall entirely rotten with scandals,
but it shines, it exudes ...

QUITE A DIFFERENT WALL

A wall, quite a different wall, existing
for long enough only when it gets dark,
and thus mainly in the dark, a wall
of stone in the front and of bricks in the rear...

An aging man who doesn't know
where to go and would like somewhere farther,
beats it with his head and pleads:
"Give in, give in, you are not remoteness,
you are only distance! "

But it can't be coaxed to admit
that it is not at all ...

A QUESTION MARK

Indeed! So artless May
you have not experienced yet.
There are several letters
that don't need to be answered,
an open window, trees,
and behind them—a cemetery wall.
If you had to go there,
what would you have to take with you?
A small cup and an empty bottle
is enough for some. But
what about you
when even the invisible
does not see itself of its own accord?

Editorial Note

This volume of Vladimir Holan works, called Walls, contains chronologically arranged poems on the theme of a wall or walls from the following collections: